BRAGGOTS AND ALE MEADS

BREWING WITH HONEY

A Plan Bee Publication

The Book Conspiracy

© Melvyn Fickling 2020

Melvyn Fickling has asserted his rights under the Copyright, Design and Patents Act, 1988, to be identified as the author of this work.

First published digitally by The Book Conspiracy Limited in 2020.

All rights reserved. No part of this publication may be reproduced, stored in a retrieval system, or transmitted in any form or by any means, electronic, mechanical, photocopying, recording, or otherwise, without the prior permission of both the copyright owner and the above publisher of this book.

The recipes in this book and are for personal home use only. No commercial use is allowed without the express written permission of the author.

Paperback ISBN: 978-1-9997484-3-2

Author portrait by Moff Moffat

Cover art © Kate Willows   katewillows.co.uk
                                  instagram.com/katewillowsart
                                  facebook.com/KateWillowsArtist

Dedicated to Karen Sunshine with love

CONTENTS

Who will use this book?	6
A brief history	8
Types	9
Conditioning & ageing	10
Alcohol	11
Ingredients	12
Suppliers	15
Equipment	16
General methodology	20

ALE MEAD RECIPES

Bluebird – Blueberry Ale Mead	28
Blackbird – Blackberry Ale Mead	29
Virgin Queen – Cherry Ale Mead	29
Pearly Queen – Mint & Tea Ale Mead	30
Perry Jack – Pear Ale Mead	32
Spring Queen – Elderflower Ale Mead	34
Gin Palace (version 1) – Sloe Gin Ale Mead	36
Gin Palace (version 2) – Juniper & Liquorice Ale Mead	38

DOUBLE ALE MEAD RECIPES

Bitefinger – Sloe Double Ale Mead	42
Scurvy Dog – Lime Double Ale Mead	44
Grape Shot – Grape Double Ale Mead	46

TRIPLE ALE MEAD RECIPES

Honey Moon – Simple Triple Ale Mead	50
Strawberry Valentine – Strawberry Triple Ale Mead	52
Christmas Queen – Festive Triple Ale Mead	54

BRAGGOT RECIPES

Ginger Queen – Light Ginger Braggot	58
Bloody Mary – Light Cherry Braggot	60
Lumber Jack – Light Maple Braggot	62
Jack o' the Green – Light Greengage Braggot	64
Hallowe'en Jack – Apple Wheat Braggot	66
Nelson's Victory – Medium Oaked Braggot	68
Jack Tar – Dark Liquorice Braggot	70

DOUBLE BRAGGOT RECIPES

May Queen – Elderflower Double Light Braggot	74
Wicker Man – Greengage Double Light Braggot	76
Queen of Scots – Double Light Braggot	78
Gun Decks – Double Dark Braggot	80

SESSION BRAGGOT RECIPES

Black Jack – Extra Dark Session Braggot	84
Ginger Tom – Light Session Braggot	86
Green Man – Greengage Light Session Braggot	88
Jack Bracket – Apple Light Session Braggot	90
Carnival Queen – Elderflower Wheat Session Braggot	92
The Nelson Touch – Medium Rum & Cloves Session Braggot	94

Who will use this recipe book and why they will like it

The brewing novice – These are people who might have brewed something when they were younger or have always thought brewing might be a cool thing to try. Generally, these would-be brewers buy a commercially packaged brewing kit of a style of beer, or even a specifically named example of a beer style, that they know they will enjoy. These kits contain the three basic ingredients they need to produce cheap palatable beer in a sufficient quantity to keep them in a refreshed state for a few weeks or more.

The recipes presented here are no more difficult to follow than the average brewing kit, although shopping for the ingredients separately may be a slight inconvenience. The Ale Meads and Braggots these instructions lead you to produce are in many cases far finer than most generic, beer-in-a-box supermarket bargains.

The mead maker – There is a surprisingly vibrant and growing band of makers who produce traditional mead at home. Mead is generally fermented with wine yeast and produced in much the same way as wine. It is a very fine drink once it has matured long enough in the bottle, but this may take several years and, in many cases, it can take over a decade for a specialist mead to reach its peak condition. The Ale Meads and Braggots described in this book are produced in a similar way to most standard beer styles. Once bottled, the lower strength variants will be ready to consume within three months, their stronger cousins within six months. The mead maker will enjoy tinkering with the recipes in this book and, I hope, will appreciate the ready availability of a glass of honeyed brew to enjoy while they watch their traditional mead maturing over the fullness of time.

The accomplished home brewer – I have limited the Braggot recipes in this book to the use of malt extract in place of whole malted grains, purely for the sake of simplicity. Full grain brewing is a complex and engrossing process which gives the brewer full control over the nuances of body and flavour that appear in the finished product. It's my hope that all-grain brewers will seize the opportunity to experiment with their own variations on my recipes; where I specify light malt extract, they might use a light ale malt bill that has given them good results in the past, where I specify dark malt extract, they might substitute their favourite porter or stout malt bill.

As you'll discover, Ale Meads do not have any appreciable malt additions, so this new branch of brewing will bring something fresh to the repertoire of every homebrewer, whatever their level of experience.

The very brief history of honey and alcohol

The history of alcoholic beverages probably began with an accidental encounter between some left-over honey in a bowl and a shower of rainwater that contained natural, air-borne yeasts. This happy accident gave rise to something that we might call "feral ale mead". Exactly where and when this happened is lost in the unchartered depths of pre-history. But there is anecdotal evidence to suggest that European production of fermented honey beverages was part of human society in 2,000 BC or earlier. Mead (essentially Honey Wine) has since played a role in the myths and legends of most European cultures, most notably Germanic, Norse and Celtic.

It's likely that Mead Ales were commonplace and popular in Britain up to the period of The Napoleonic Wars. One version was probably prepared directly at the bar, or in the hostelry kitchen, by blending Mead wine and ordinary ale in roughly equal quantities, sometimes with the addition of various spices. They were almost certainly also brewed as a discreet entity, with honey being added to the ale wort at varying stages during the boil or the fermentation.

Types of Ale Mead and Braggot

Ale Meads rely wholly upon honey to supply the fermentable sugars. In some recipes, small amounts of malted grain are steeped in the water to add colour. Ale Meads are hopped in the same way as lighter ales or lagers and flavoured with natural ingredients. Alcoholic strength depends on the quantity of honey used per imperial gallon;
Ale Mead – One pound of honey per imperial gallon – approx. 4.2% abv;
Double Ale Mead – Two pounds of honey per imperial gallon – approx. 7.4% abv;
Triple Ale Mead – Three pounds of honey per imperial gallon – approx. 10.5% abv.

Braggot is traditionally brewed using roughly equal amounts of malt and honey to supply the fermentable sugars. Some Braggots are hopped in the same way as ales and flavoured with natural ingredients. The nature of the finished drink is heavily dependent upon the type of malt extract employed; light, medium or dark. Alcoholic strength depends on the quantity of honey used per imperial gallon;
Braggot – One pound of honey and 500g of malt extract per imperial gallon – approx. 8.5% abv;
Double Braggot – Two pounds of honey and 500g of malt extract per imperial gallon – approx. 10.5% abv;
Session Braggot – These are lower strength variants where standard Braggot recipes are adjusted to deliver the signature flavour of the original at a lower strength – approx. 4.5% abv.

Conditioning and ageing

Note: All the recipes in this book are intended for bottling.

Conditioning is an essential process that gives your bottled ales their natural sparkle and head. Essentially, once fermentation is complete (meaning all fermentable sugars have been consumed by the yeast), your ale is ready for bottling. As part of the bottling process we add a small amount of fresh fermentable sugar (we'll look at this whole process in more detail in the section entitled Methodology). This new sugar wakes up the yeast and a small level of fermentation is achieved in the bottle, producing a desirable and attractive degree of carbonisation.

The minimum conditioning period is two months. Stronger ale in the region of 7 to 8% will benefit from 6 to 9 months conditioning. Ale of around 11% or above will benefit from up to 12 months of conditioning.

Ageing is a slightly different prospect. Ageing involves the cellaring of a conditioned ale for a longer period of time to allow the ale an opportunity to develop further its particular characteristics. Ageing will always *change* the character of an ale; it is a question of taste and circumstance whether it *improves* that character.

Conditioned ales of 5 to 7.5% may be aged for a suggested maximum of two years;

Conditioned ales of 7.5 to 10% may be aged for 5 to 10 years;

Conditioned ales over 10% may be aged for 10 years or more.

When ageing your brews, bottles must be stored upright in the dark at a near-constant cool temperature. Remember that ageing carries as much chance of spoiling a good ale as turning it into something truly wonderful. Ageing is always attempted at your own risk.

Alcohol – Treat it with respect

It is my personal experience that alcohol brewed from honey delivers its own special feeling of well-being. However, it must always be remembered that consumption of any kind of alcohol carries significant health risks. Typically, these risks increase with the quantity drunk and the strength of your chosen libation.

You may have noted that some of the variants I am inviting you to brew carry a premium alcohol content. Caution should therefore be applied to their consumption.

A system based on "units" has been devised to enable you to evaluate your alcohol consumption and manage it in line with the health guidance issued by the government from time to time.

At the time of writing the UK government's advice is to limit alcohol consumption to 14 units per week (nominally 2 units per day) regardless of gender.

In real terms a unit is 10ml of pure alcohol. Translating that to what might be contained in a pint of beer or a glass of wine is where most people's understanding unravels. But the maths isn't too difficult, as long as you've measured the strength of your brew (covered in the section entitled Methodology) and you know the capacity of the bottle that contains it.

Let's say you've made a 7.5% Braggot and conditioned it in 330ml bottles. We know that the alcohol takes up 7.5% of the container (remember abv stands for alcohol by volume).

So, 7.5% of 330ml = 24.75ml

We know that one unit is 10ml, so our bottle of Braggot contains just shy of 2.5 units, thereby exceeding our nominal daily allowance.

Apply the same maths to a 5% Ale Mead in the same size of bottle:

5% of 330ml = 16.5ml

So, the Ale Mead contains slightly less than 1.7 units, comfortably within the nominal daily allowance.

If in doubt about alcohol, its effects and the potential harm it might do to your health and lifestyle, do not drink beverages that contain it.

Ingredients

Honey – In these recipes, we are using honey as a naturally flavoured sugar. In the act of boiling the honey (even if only for a short time) we are changing the nature of those flavours. As might be expected, it is the more delicate nuances present in the finer, more expensive honeys, that are lost most easily. It is for this reason that I suggest using jars of standard honey that are easily found in your local supermarket. I add a jar or two of honey to my shopping basket on every visit, so when the need to brew overtakes me, I always have a decent stock.
I use set honey, only because I find it easier to handle and there is less chance of a messy spill. The standard jar available in the UK contains 454g, which is the equivalent of one imperial pound. All recipes call for honey in full-jar units. If the honey available where you live comes in 500g jars, the recipes will deliver a slightly higher alcohol content.
It is of course cheaper to buy honey in larger, catering style, containers, as long as you don't mind measuring out the quantity you require for each brewing session.

Malt – All types of malt are produced by carefully managing the natural germination process of cereal grains. In the brewing business that cereal is predominantly barley, although wheat is also malted in significant quantities. The harvested crop is delivered to a special processing plant called a Maltings. After a careful cleaning process, the grains are spread into a thin layer in large, specially equipped rooms and encouraged to germinate by the introduction of moisture and warmth. The natural purpose of cereal grains, as with any seed, is to develop and grow into a new plant. Rain and sunshine are the triggers for that in the natural world, and it is these natural elements that are mimicked on the malting room floor. Once germination starts, the grain begins converting the starches it contains into sugars to feed the development of the new plant. These are the sugars that we need to obtain for the fermentation process.

When it's judged to be the optimum time (typically when the beginnings of roots appear) the germination process is halted by air-drying and then kilning the malted grain. During the last part of kilning the temperature is raised to cure the malt and to give it its colour. The longer it is kilned, the darker it gets.

Commercial breweries and committed home-enthusiasts use these malted grains as their raw material. They steep the grains in hot water to extract the sugars. The resultant sweet liquid is called the wort, its colour will reflect the lightness or darkness of the malt mixture used to make it. The wort is boiled together with hops, then cooled and fermented with yeast to make beer.

Producing good wort on any scale requires a level of skill and a close attention to detail. For ease and convenience for the average homebrewer, the recipes in this book use malt extract. Simply put, a production facility carries out the production of the wort, then condenses it to produce liquid malt extract (LME), or further condenses and dries it to produce dried malt extract (DME), often called Spray Malt after the drying method.

My braggot recipes are built around dried malt extract, as I find this most convenient to store and less messy to use. DME is generally available in 500g bags, 1kg bags or 25kg bags. All braggot recipes in this book are formulated to use 1kg of extract.

DME comes in light, medium, dark and extra dark. A variant made from malted wheat is also available.

Malted and Roasted Grains – Although DME is the mainstay of our ingredients (together with honey), we can use malted or roasted barley to add a depth of colour to some of the brews. This is done by steeping a muslin bag of grains in hot water for a period before the start of the boil. The grains specified in some of the recipes are crystal malt, black malt, or roasted barley.

Hops – The addition of hops stamps the unmistakable character of beer on these drinks and gives them a satisfying depth of finish on the palate.

Generally, in the lighter recipes I use lager hops, in the more robust recipes I opt for more traditional ale hops.

If you are an adventurous spirit, I'd encourage you to experiment with the ever-increasing range of hop varieties that are available, now most are sold in conveniently small 100g packs.

Yeast – Dried yeast is the living engine of fermentation. This single-celled fungus feeds on sugars while producing alcohol and carbon dioxide as by-products. While the sugar source lasts, yeast will feed and reproduce. When the sugar source is depleted, the yeast will go dormant and sink to the bottom of the vessel, signalling the end of fermentation. When your brew is primed with a touch more sugar on bottling day, they will spring back to life to create the carbonation in the bottle that gives the sparkle to your brew.

We will be using three basic types of dried yeast: ale yeast, sparkling wine yeast and cider yeast. All yeast has a tolerance ceiling for the alcohol concentration in its environment. So, although ale yeast is our regular workhorse, where we expect a high alcohol level, we'll use sparkling wine yeast (sometimes labelled as champagne yeast), or even a mixture of ale and wine yeasts together.

When apples are involved in the recipe, I tend to use a mix of cider yeast and ale yeast.

Additives Natural – One of the major joys of brewing with honey is its happy compatibility with the addition of fruits and spices: elderflower (dried or foraged fresh), exotic and hedgerow fruits, chopped liquorice root, fresh ginger, oak chips and Christmas spices all make their appearance within these pages.

Additives Processed – I use only two things that fall into this category: yeast nutrient (because, let's face it, they do work hard) and brewing sugar (for priming at the bottling stage).

Suppliers

Much of what you need will be available via your local home-brew shop, should you be lucky enough to live near one.

If you need, or prefer, to buy online, these UK suppliers are recommended:

For DMEs, malted grains, hops, yeast, brewing equipment, cleaning equipment and most sundries – **home-brew-hopshop.co.uk** or **themaltmiller.co.uk**

For natural additives that you might not find in your supermarket or greengrocer – **healthysupplies.co.uk** or **justingredients.co.uk** usually have what you need between them.

Equipment

Stock Pot – You'll need a sturdy stainless-steel stock pot. As all the recipes begin with 8 litres of fresh water, I strongly suggest that a 20-litre pot is the minimum you should consider. This gives plenty of spare capacity which keeps the possibility of spills and splashes of the hot wort to a minimum.

Electronic Scales – Good quality kitchen scales that are accurate are essential. If you're a cook, you probably already have these.

Electronic Timer – You almost certainly have one on your phone, but you might want to invest in a stand-alone kitchen timer considering the proximity of sticky ingredients and large volumes of water.

Muslin Bags – Have a few of these to hand. They can be washed and used several times. Generally available in hardware stores or kitchenware shops.

Cooking Thermometer – Look for one with a metal clip that attaches to the lip of the pot. Another purchase from the kitchenware shop.

Spoons – Buy a good wooden spoon and reserve it for brewing purposes. You'll also need a standard dessert spoon to scoop the honey out of the jars.

Sterilising Agents – Cleanliness is key to avoid infections that can taint your brews. Suitable no-rinse agents are available from homebrew shops and websites. These can be made up into sprays for maximum convenience. Boxes of tablets sold in supermarkets and chemists for sterilising baby feeding equipment are useful to soak airlocks, bungs, grommets and, when made up in a larger container, empty bottles.

Fine Sieve – Used to remove hops and other materials as you transfer the cooled wort to the fermentation vessel.

Jugs – A couple of one-litre capacity jugs should always be within reach.

Funnels – A few small plastic funnels are always useful, especially if you are using demi-johns with narrow necks as fermentation vessels.

Orange Squeezer – Extracted juice is used for acidity.

Fermentation Vessels – Glass demi-johns or carboys are a traditional candidate for home fermenting. Typically, they are one-gallon capacity which requires the use of two or more for the batch sizes suggested in this book. Also, their narrow necks are awkward when using fruit and they are sometimes difficult to clean without a specialist cleaning brush. I prefer to use plastic fermenting vessels with wide mouths and a screw-on lid pre-fitted with a grommet to take an airlock, 10 litre capacity for two-gallon brews and 22 litre capacity for larger batches. Plastic fermentation buckets with fitted lids drilled for an airlock are also available in suitable capacities.

Airlock – I recommend bubbler style airlocks. These have an S-shaped tube with spherical bulges, a bit like a small snake that's swallowed several gobstoppers, that holds a small amount of water through which the escaping gas bubbles. A smaller style of airlock is available which employs a separate "top-hat" element that floats in a small reservoir of water, rising and falling as the gas escapes. This type of airlock tends to dry out if not tended to, and a particularly vigorous fermentation can eject the top-hat completely and allow air into the vessel. The cost difference between the two is small, so plump for bubblers if you can.

Siphon – Food grade tubing will be needed to siphon the finished brew from fermentation vessel to bottling bucket (I use a 25-litre fermenting bucket for bottling). Sucking through the brew to prime the siphon adds a small chance of infecting the brew. Easy-to-use auto-siphons (which prime with the aid of a manual pump action) are available and are more hygienic.

Hydrometer and Trial Jar – These are required to take the original gravity and final gravity of your brew so the alcohol content (the specific gravity) can be calculated. In simple terms, a hydrometer measures the density of a liquid. Prior to fermentation your brew is packed with dense sugars which cause the hydrometer to float higher than it would in plain water. Once fully fermented, most of the sugar turns to alcohol which is less dense than the sugar it was converted from, so the hydrometer rides lower in the liquid. Taking both readings from the calibrated stem of the hydrometer allows the alcohol content to be calculated.

How to calculate ABV: Original Gravity minus Final Gravity
For example: 1.032 – 1.000 = 0.032
Multiply by 105:   0.032 x 105 = 3.36
This expresses the percentage of alcohol by *weight*
Multiply by 1.25:   3.36 x 1.25 = 4.2
This expresses the percentage of alcohol by volume (ABV)

You might question whether this procedure is necessary for a homebrewer who follows the recipe, as each recipe is labelled with the ABV it is likely to produce. I would caution you that taking a final gravity reading is the only way to be *absolutely* sure that a fermentation has reached its end. If you bottle a brew that has an appreciable quantity of unfermented sugars present, you will probably suffer messy and potentially dangerous "bottle-bombs" when the brew continues to ferment after it's capped and the increasing pressure shatters the glass. Note: You need *both* readings to accurately calculate alcohol content.

Bottles – Your available stock of empty bottles can become a limiting factor for your brewing activities, especially if you are making the stronger styles that need the longest conditioning. You'll need 330ml capacity for most recipes and 500ml capacity for the Session Braggots. Always use green or brown glass (never clear glass). Low cost, screw-top plastic (PET) bottles are available. I'm not a fan of these on aesthetic grounds, but they can be a useful backup in an emergency.

It should be possible to find a friendly pub of café that will allow you to sort through their empties before they go to glass recycling. These foraged treasures will need to be soaked to get the labels off. Experience will tell you which brands have the least aggressive label adhesive.

If you can't scavenge enough suitable bottles, you can always buy new stock in. Try JBConline.co.uk for UK deliveries.

Crown Capper – Various styles of capper are available to seal off your bottled brew, including some hand-held types. I would suggest you go straight for a proper bench-capper. This comprises a base that supports a post with the capping device on an adjustable ratchet to match various heights of bottle. Once set to the bottle size you are using, a new crown cap is placed in the magnetic holder and a firm pull of the lever crimps the cap over the mouth of the bottle. The base of a bench capper often has screw-holes to fix it to a bench. Obviously, you won't want to do this in your kitchen, but I've found it helps with stability if you screw it to an old breadboard to increase its footprint.

New caps are available in various colours from homebrew shops and websites. Buy in bulk.

Labels – There are quite a few programs available for designing and printing labels. How far you go with this is up to you. Personally, I just mark the bottle-cap with an indelible sharpie (e.g. GQ for Ginger Queen) and mark the full name and bottling date on the storage box.

Notebook – Always write down what you're bottling, the out-turn and the bottled-on date. We've provided a few pages at the back of this book to get you started.

General Methodology

Take a few moments to read through the recipe you have chosen to brew. Weigh out the ingredients that you need into bowls and have them close-by.
If the recipe calls for fruit additions, make sure to rinse the fruit well under running water prior to use. If you're using fruit you've previously frozen, you would've rinsed well prior to freezing. Commercially frozen produce can be considered clean from the packet.

Measure fresh tap water into your stockpot. All the recipes call for 8 litres. Turn on your hob. If the recipe calls for steeped malt grains, set up your thermometer and keep an eye on the rising temperature. If no steeping is needed, proceed at full heat until the water is boiling.

If steeping malt grains is required, weigh the grains into the muslin bag. These bags are generally long, sock-like objects, sewn or tied-off at one end. Once your grains are weighed in, tie off the other end with a simple knot and push a wooden spoon handle through the knot. This allows you to rest the wooden spoon across the top of the pot and suspend the grains in the water. Once the water has reached the correct temperature, adjust the heat to maintain it, submerge the muslin bag and set your timer.
When you've removed the steeped grains, your water can technically be called wort. Bring the wort to the boil.
For Ale Meads you will now introduce the first hop addition. For Braggots you will introduce the first hops and the spray malt. Take care when adding spray malt to avoid splashing. Stir carefully, bring back to the boil and set your timer.

When the boil time expires, turn off the heat (flame out). We are about to add the honey. We turn off the heat to avoid the honey sinking to the bottom and scorching in the direct heat.

I find set honey easier to use. I hold a metal dessert spoon with its bowl in the hot wort for a few moments. The warmed spoon makes it easier to scoop the set honey from the jar into the pot. Again, be careful to avoid splashes in the hot liquid. Once all the honey is added, stir carefully until it is completely dissolved. Add any other ingredients the recipe specifies, then bring back to the boil and set your timer.

When the boil time expires, introduce the second hop addition. Maintain the boil and set your timer.

Once the boil is finished the wort needs to cool completely. From this point on, the wort is susceptible to infection, so at the very least, fit the lid to deter flying insects. Hastening the cooling is a smart thing to do. A 20-litre capacity stockpot will fit in the stainless-steel sink found in most kitchens. Fill the sink around the pot with cold water, taking care that the pot doesn't float and tip. Changing the water two or three times over the course of 20 minutes should bring the temperature of the wort down nicely. Take care when changing the water in the sink, especially the first time, as it gets quite hot.

Everything that comes into contact with the wort from now on *must* be sterile. That includes the jug you transfer the liquid with, the sieve you pour it through to remove the hops *and* the fermentation vessel it goes into.

Juice the oranges (using a washed and sterilised juicer) and pour the juice into the fermentation vessel. Add a teaspoon of yeast nutrient as well. The citric acid and the nutrients are essential for the optimal health of the brew. Yeast nutrient is available online and from homebrew shops and looks very much like granulated sugar. Citric acid is also available in granule form, but I prefer to use natural juice.
Note: Don't be tempted to use lemons as a source of acid, they are much more intrusive in the flavour profile of the finished product.

Strain the cooled wort through the sieve into the fermentation vessel. Things are made easier if you can source a sieve that fits nicely in the mouth of the vessel. At this point in the process it is desirable to get oxygen into the wort as the yeast needs oxygen to work. The splashing and separation caused by the sieve adequately achieves this goal.

Make up the volume in the fermentation vessel to the recipe batch size with fresh water. Stir with a sterile spoon and take a sample to measure your original gravity. Record the reading in your notebook.
Note: Although fermentation vessels are generally stamped with graduations that indicate their capacity, it is well worth checking the accuracy of this scale by carefully measuring in volumes of water using a trusted measuring jug before your first use with a brew.

Add any fruits that the recipe demands.

Pitch the specified type and quantity of yeast(s), secure the lid, and fit an airlock filled sufficiently with clean water. Many yeasts are quite happy to be pitched in their dry form, to hydrate on the surface of the wort and sink down to begin their work. But always check the instructions that accompany the yeast you've purchased.

Ale yeast requires the temperature to be between 16-24 degrees centigrade to operate efficiently. Above this range and you risk the yeast producing off-flavours. Below this range and the yeast will slow down and may go dormant, again risking the health of your brew.

Fermentation will begin within 24 hours. At the beginning of the process you will notice gas bubbling through your airlock. This is carbon dioxide, one of the main by-products of fermentation (alcohol being the other). This activity will lessen over time as the yeast consumes the sugars in the wort.

Avoid the temptation to open the fermentation vessel to check on progress. Quite apart from the risk of introducing bacterial infection, oxygen is now your enemy. Too much exposure to oxygen will taint the brew. Leaving the lid and airlock undisturbed allows the accumulated carbon dioxide to form a protective blanket that excludes oxygen.

The fermentation process will generally take between 7 and 14 days. Once fermentation is complete, allow the vessel to stand for a day or two to allow the brew to clear and the sediment to accumulate at the bottom. Bear in mind you will need to syphon the brew out of the fermentation vessel into the bottling bucket, and to do so requires the vessel to be higher than the bucket. So, if you've fermented on the floor, it helps to lift the vessel up onto a sturdy work-top to let the sediment settle.

To produce a desirable carbon-dioxide sparkle in the finished brew, we need to induce a controlled fermentation when it's sealed inside the bottles. This is called conditioning. This is achieved by adding a small quantity of brewing sugar. Home brew shops sell Carbonation Drops. These have the appearance of small boiled sweets and you drop one in each of your sterilised bottles before filling and capping. This is convenient, but inflexible.

My preferred method is batch priming. Each recipe shows the recommended weight of brewing sugar to prime the batch size and style in question. Weigh this out into a jug and add a little very hot water, sufficient to dissolve the sugar completely. You will add this as the brew is siphoning into the bottling bucket.

Before you open the fermenting vessel, make sure everything is ready. All your bottles should be washed, sterilised, and drained. Your bottling jug should be clean and sterile, as should your syphon tube (draw some sterilising solution through it and then some fresh water) and your bottling bucket. Your bench-capper needs to be wiped down and checked for smooth functioning. And don't forget to check you have enough bottle-caps (it doesn't hurt to sterilise these too).

Place the bottling bucket next to, but lower than, the fermentation vessel. It should be low enough so that when all the liquid is transferred, the surface of the liquid in the bottling bucket would be below the base of the fermentation vessel. If the bucket is higher than this, the liquid will "find its level" and your syphoning will stall.

When all is ready, open the fermentation vessel and insert the syphon tube to the bottom of the container. Most syphons have a small foot that prevents sediment from entering the tube, but always move with utmost care to prevent disturbing the sediment. Make sure the other end of the syphon is safely in the bottling bucket.

Start your syphon (by pumping, if it's an auto-syphon, or sucking if it's not). As soon as the liquid starts to flow put the end of the tubing at the bottom of the bucket so the liquid flows smoothly without splashing. If it splashes or cascades, it is in danger of absorbing oxygen, which risks compromising its character.

When the bottom of the bucket is covered, slowly pour in the priming sugar solution. The slow swirl created by the flowing liquid will ensure an even mix of sugar throughout the batch.

When most of the liquid is transferred, the syphon will start to slurp air through the tube. Stop the syphoning at that point and remove the syphon tube from the bottling bucket.

Your brew is now at its most vulnerable to infection, so proceed immediately to bottling. Fill your bottling jug and pour carefully, with minimum splashing into your bottles. Fill each one to just above the shoulder, leaving a small airspace in the neck, and cap securely.

Once the brew is bottled, wipe down the bottles with a damp cloth (to deter ants invading your bottle store) and mark for identification in your preferred fashion. Place in boxes or crates and mark the container with the brew's name and bottling date. Record the same information in your notebook along with the out-turn (number of full bottles produced).

From now on your bottles must remain upright until you eventually come to consume the contents. The first step is conditioning, the recipe will note the recommended time period.

As conditioning is simply a small bout of fermentation, it follows that it needs the same temperature range of 16-24 degrees centigrade to take place properly. I suggest you condition somewhere in your house, away from hot spots like radiators, and preferably in the dark. Your garage may well get too hot in the summer and too cold in the winter but may well be suitable in spring and autumn. I have re-purposed a downstairs WC to be an indoor bottle-store, but I realise this may be a luxury!

I strongly recommend you attempt to age at least a few bottles of various brews, especially the stronger recipes, just for the fun of the experiment. Ageing needs more consistently cool conditions and requires your storage area to be dark. If you are lucky enough to have a cellar (or know someone who has), this is an adventure you should not miss.

Once your batch reaches the end of the recommended conditioning period, it's time to enjoy the fruits of your labour. Chill slightly in the fridge (bottles standing upright), pop the cap and pour carefully into a clean glass with a single smooth motion. Watch for any sediment and avoid getting it into the glass.

Sit back and enjoy.

Final thoughts - Be mindful always of your safety. Brewing engages you with very hot water over considerable time periods. Never brew when drunk or otherwise distracted. And be mindful of your health. Enjoy these distinctive concoctions in moderation. Cheers!

ALE MEADS

Bluebird – Blueberry Ale Mead

Batch size: Two Imperial Gallons   Expect: Original Gravity 1.032
                                      Final Gravity   1.000
                                      ABV   4.2%

Bring 8 litres of water to the boil

Add 20g of Hallertauer Hersbrucker hops – Boil for 25 minutes

Flame out

Add **2** x 454g of honey – Stir carefully to dissolve – Re-light the flame and bring back to the boil

Add 10g of Hallertauer Mittelfrüh hops – Boil for 5 minutes

Flame out

Cool wort to 20°c or lower

Pour the juice of two oranges into the fermenting vessel(s) and add yeast nutrient

Strain cooled wort into fermenting vessel(s) and make up to 2 gallons with fresh water

Stir and take a sample for measurement of original gravity

Add 1kg of fresh or frozen blueberries – if using fresh berries, chop them roughly

Pitch 2g of ale yeast and fit an airlock

When fermentation is complete, allow the vessel to stand for a day or two to allow the brew to clear

When clear, rack into bottling bucket and batch prime with **80g** of brewing sugar
Transfer to 28 x 330ml bottles

Condition for two months at room temperature

***

Variations:

Blackbird – Blackberry Ale Mead

Substitute 1kg of blueberries with 1kg blackberries

Virgin Queen – Cherry Ale Mead

Substitute 1 kg blueberries with 1kg cherries – if using fresh cherries, slash them with a knife

Pearly Queen – Mint and Tea Ale Mead

This was inspired by a friend's mint and tea recipe for wine. I was sceptical until he offered me a glass. Adjust the mint to taste.

Batch size: Two Imperial Gallons

Expect: Original Gravity 1.032
Final Gravity 1.000
ABV 4.2%

Heat 8 litres of water to 70°c and maintain temperature

Place 100g of light crystal malt in a muslin bag – Suspend the bag in the hot water and steep for 30 minutes

Remove malt bag and bring the wort to the boil

Add 20g of Hallertauer Hersbrucker hops – Boil for 25 minutes

Flame out

Add **2** x 454g of honey – Stir carefully to dissolve – Re-light the flame and bring back to the boil

Add 3 pints of bruised mint leaves – Boil for 5 minutes

Place 4 x English Breakfast tea bags in a muslin bag and suspend the bag in the boiling wort
Add 10g of Hallertauer Mittelfrüh hops – Boil for 5 minutes

Flame out – Remove the bag containing the tea

Cool wort to 20°c or lower

Pour the juice of two oranges into the fermenting vessel(s) and add yeast nutrient

Strain cooled wort into fermenting vessel(s) and make up to 2 gallons with fresh water

Stir and take a sample for measurement of original gravity

Pitch 2g of ale yeast and fit an airlock

***

When fermentation is complete, allow the vessel to stand for a day or two to allow the brew to clear

When clear, rack into bottling bucket and batch prime with **80g** of brewing sugar
Transfer to 28 x 330ml bottles

Condition for two months at room temperature

Perry Jack – Pear Ale Mead

Batch size: Two Imperial Gallons   Expect: Original Gravity 1.032
                                          Final Gravity   1.000
                                          ABV   4.2%

Heat 8 litres of water to 70°c and maintain temperature

Place 100g of light crystal malt in a muslin bag – Suspend the bag in the hot water and steep for 30 minutes

Remove malt bag and bring the wort to the boil

Add 20g of Nugget hops – Boil for 25 minutes

Flame out

Add **2** x 454g of honey – Stir carefully to dissolve – Re-light the flame and bring back to the boil

Add 10g of Nugget hops – Boil for 5 minutes

Flame out

Cool wort to 20°c or lower

Pour the juice of two oranges into the fermenting vessel(s) and add yeast nutrient

Strain cooled wort into fermenting vessel(s) and make up to 2 gallons with fresh water

Stir and take a sample for measurement of original gravity

Add 12 x Conference pears washed and sliced

Pitch 1g of ale yeast and 1g of cider yeast - fit an airlock

***

When fermentation is complete, allow the vessel to stand for a day or two to allow the brew to clear

When clear, rack into bottling bucket and batch prime with **80g** of brewing sugar
Transfer to 28 x 330ml bottles

Condition for two months at room temperature

Spring Queen – Elderflower Ale Mead

Batch size: Two Imperial Gallons   Expect: Original Gravity   1.032
                                        Final Gravity   1.000
                                        ABV   4.2%

Heat 8 litres of water to 70°c and maintain temperature

Place 100g of light crystal malt in a muslin bag – Suspend the bag in the hot water and steep for 30 minutes

Remove malt bag and bring the wort to the boil

Add 20g of Hallertauer Hersbrucker hops – Boil for 25 minutes

Flame out

Add **2** x 454g of honey – Stir carefully to dissolve – Re-light the flame and bring back to the boil

Add 20g dried elderflower – Boil for 15 minutes

Add 10g of Hallertauer Mittelfrüh hops – Boil for 5 minutes

Flame out

Cool wort to 20°c or lower

Steep 10g dried elderflower in a small bowl of just-boiled water for 20 minutes – Strain the liquid into the fermenting vessel(s)

Pour the juice of two oranges into the fermenting vessel(s) and add yeast nutrient

Strain cooled wort into fermenting vessel(s) and make up to 2 gallons with fresh water

Stir and take a sample for measurement of original gravity

Pitch 2g of ale yeast and fit an airlock

***

When fermentation is complete, allow the vessel to stand for a day or two to allow the brew to clear

When clear, rack into bottling bucket and batch prime with **80g** of brewing sugar
Transfer to 28 x 330ml bottles

Condition for two months at room temperature

***

Variation: Omit dried elderflower. De-stem three pints of freshly picked elderflowers and place in the bottom of the fermenting vessel(s) with the orange juice and nutrients. Do not cool the wort. Instead, carefully strain the just-boiled wort onto the elderflowers.
Close the vessel(s) under airlock while the wort cools naturally – this may take a few hours.
When the wort has cooled to 20°c or lower, stir and take a sample for measurement of original gravity, pitch the yeast and proceed as described above.

Gin Palace (version 1) – Sloe Gin Ale Mead

This recipe calls for sloe berries that have already been used to produce sloe gin. When you've bottled off your sloe gin, salvage the berries and freeze them ready for brew day.

Batch size: Two Imperial Gallons

Expect: Original Gravity 1.032
Final Gravity 0.995
ABV 4.8%

Heat 8 litres of water to 70°c and maintain temperature

Place 100g of light crystal malt in a muslin bag – Suspend the bag in the hot water and steep for 30 minutes

Remove malt bag and bring the wort to the boil

Add 20g of Hallertauer Hersbrucker hops – Boil for 25 minutes

Flame out

Add **2** x 454g of honey – Stir carefully to dissolve – Re-light the flame and bring back to the boil

Add 10g of Hallertauer Mittelfrüh hops – Boil for 5 minutes

Flame out

Cool wort to 20°c or lower

Pour the juice of two oranges into the fermenting vessel(s) and add yeast nutrient

Strain cooled wort into fermenting vessel(s) and make up to 2 gallons with fresh water

Stir and take a sample for measurement of original gravity

Add 1kg of gin-soaked sloes

Pitch 2g of ale yeast and fit an airlock

***

When fermentation is complete, allow the vessel to stand for a day or two to allow the brew to clear

When clear, rack into bottling bucket and batch prime with **80g** of brewing sugar
Transfer to 28 x 330ml bottles

Condition for two months at room temperature

Gin Palace (version 2) – Juniper and Liquorice Ale Mead

This recipe replicates the nuance of gin by incorporating its main botanical adjunct.

Batch size: Two Imperial Gallons   Expect: Original Gravity 1.032
                                       Final Gravity   1.000
                                       ABV   4.2%

Heat 8 litres of water to 70°c and maintain temperature

Place 100g of light crystal malt in a muslin bag – Suspend the bag in the hot water and steep for 30 minutes

Remove malt bag and bring the wort to the boil

Add 20g of Hallertauer Hersbrucker hops – Boil for 25 minutes

Flame out

Add **2** x 454g of honey – Stir carefully to dissolve – Re-light the flame and bring back to the boil

Add 250g dried juniper berries and 25g chopped liquorice root – Boil for 15 minutes

Add 10g of Hallertauer Mittelfrüh hops – Boil for 5 minutes

Flame out

Cool wort to 20°c or lower

Pour the juice of two oranges into the fermenting vessel(s) and add yeast nutrient

Strain cooled wort into fermenting vessel(s) and make up to 2 gallons with fresh water

Stir and take a sample for measurement of original gravity

Pitch 2g of ale yeast and fit an airlock

***

When fermentation is complete, allow the vessel to stand for a day or two to allow the brew to clear

When clear, rack into bottling bucket and batch prime with **80g** of brewing sugar
Transfer to 28 x 330ml bottles

Condition for two months at room temperature

DOUBLE ALE MEADS

Bitefinger – Sloe Double Ale Mead

This recipe calls for sloe berries in their raw, natural state. They meld better if you slash each berry with a knife and place your harvest in the freezer for a few days. Sloe berries give this ale mead a distinctly sour flavour.

Batch size: Two Imperial Gallons   Expect: Original Gravity 1.060
                                          Final Gravity   1.004
                                          ABV   7.4%

Bring 8 litres of water to the boil

Add 20g of Hallertauer Hersbrucker hops – Boil for 25 minutes

Flame out

Add **4** x 454g of honey – Stir carefully to dissolve – Re-light the flame and bring back to the boil

Add 10g of Hallertauer Mittelfrüh hops – Boil for 5 minutes

Flame out

Cool wort to 20°c or lower

Pour the juice of two oranges into the fermenting vessel(s) and add yeast nutrient

Strain cooled wort into fermenting vessel(s) and make up to 2 gallons with fresh water

Stir and take a sample for measurement of original gravity

Add 2kg sloe berries

Pitch 2g of ale yeast and fit an airlock

***

When fermentation is complete, allow the vessel to stand for a day or two to allow the brew to clear

When clear, rack into bottling bucket and batch prime with **64g** of brewing sugar
Transfer to 28 x 330ml bottles

Condition for two months at room temperature, then four months at cellar temperature

Scurvy Dog – Lime Double Ale Mead

Batch size: Two Imperial Gallons   Expect: Original Gravity 1.060
                                        Final Gravity   1.004
                                        ABV   7.4%

Heat 8 litres of water to 70°c and maintain temperature

Place 100g of light crystal malt in a muslin bag – Suspend the bag in the hot water and steep for 30 minutes

Remove malt bag and bring the wort to the boil

Add 20g of Atlas hops – Boil for 25 minutes

Flame out

Add **4** x 454g of honey – Stir carefully to dissolve – Re-light the flame and bring back to the boil

Add 10g of Amarillo hops – Boil for 5 minutes

Flame out

Cool wort to 20°c or lower

Pour the juice of two oranges into the fermenting vessel(s) and add yeast nutrient

Pour the juice of six limes into the fermenting vessel(s)

Strain cooled wort into fermenting vessel(s) and make up to 2 gallons with fresh water

Stir and take a sample for measurement of original gravity

Pitch 2g of ale yeast and fit an airlock

***

When fermentation is complete, allow the vessel to stand for a day or two to allow the brew to clear

When clear, rack into bottling bucket and batch prime with **64g** of brewing sugar
Transfer to 28 x 330ml bottles

Condition for two months at room temperature, then four months at cellar temperature

Grape Shot – Grape Double Ale Mead

Batch size: Two Imperial Gallons

Expect: Original Gravity 1.060
Final Gravity 1.004
ABV 7.4%

Heat 8 litres of water to 70°c and maintain temperature

Place 100g of light crystal malt in a muslin bag – Suspend the bag in the hot water and steep for 30 minutes

Remove malt bag and bring the wort to the boil

Add 20g of Hallertauer Hersbrucker hops – Boil for 25 minutes

Flame out

Add **4** x 454g of honey – Stir carefully to dissolve – Re-light the flame and bring back to the boil

Add 10g of Hallertauer Mittelfrüh hops – Boil for 5 minutes

Flame out

Cool wort to 20°c or lower

Pour the juice of two oranges into the fermenting vessel(s) and add yeast nutrient

Strain cooled wort into fermenting vessel(s) and make up to 2 gallons with fresh water

Stir and take a sample for measurement of original gravity

Add 2kg halved white grapes

Pitch 2g of ale yeast and fit an airlock

***

When fermentation is complete, allow the vessel to stand for a day or two to allow the brew to clear

When clear, rack into bottling bucket and batch prime with **64g** of brewing sugar
Transfer to 28 x 330ml bottles

Condition for two months at room temperature, then four months at cellar temperature

TRIPLE ALE MEADS

Honey Moon – Simple Triple Ale Mead

This is the simplest and possibly the finest expression of an Ale Mead. Store this correctly for long enough and it will reward you with a character reminiscent of a demi-sec sparkling wine.

Batch size: Two Imperial Gallons

Expect: Original Gravity 1.084
Final Gravity 1.004
ABV 10.5%

Bring 8 litres of water to the boil

Add 25g of Hallertauer Hersbrucker hops – Boil for 25 minutes

Flame out

Add **6** x 454g of honey – Stir carefully to dissolve – Re-light the flame and bring back to the boil

Add 15g of Hallertauer Mittelfrüh hops – Boil for 5 minutes

Flame out

Cool wort to 20°c or lower

Pour the juice of two oranges into the fermenting vessel(s) and add yeast nutrient

Strain cooled wort into fermenting vessel(s) and make up to 2 gallons with fresh water

Stir and take a sample for measurement of original gravity

Pitch 1g of ale yeast and 1g of sparkling wine or champagne yeast - fit an airlock

***

When fermentation is complete, allow the vessel to stand for a day or two to allow the brew to clear

When clear, rack into bottling bucket and batch prime with **64g** of brewing sugar
Transfer to 28 x 330ml bottles

Condition for two months at room temperature, then seven months at cellar temperature

Strawberry Valentine – Strawberry Triple Ale Mead

It's notoriously difficult to obtain an authentic strawberry flavour from whole fruit, due mainly to the volume required, to say nothing of the very messy residue left behind in your FV. Commercially available strawberry cocktail juice is useful due to its concentrated nature. Or plan to brew during the annual strawberry glut and run a big batch of fruit through a juicer.

Batch size: Two Imperial Gallons

Expect: Original Gravity 1.084
Final Gravity 1.004
ABV 10.5%

Bring 8 litres of water to the boil

Add 25g of Hallertauer Hersbrucker hops – Boil for 25 minutes

Flame out

Add **6** x 454g of honey – Stir carefully to dissolve – Re-light the flame and bring back to the boil

Add 15g of Hallertauer Mittelfrüh hops – Boil for 5 minutes

Flame out

Cool wort to 20°c or lower

Pour the juice of two oranges into the fermenting vessel(s) and add yeast nutrient

Pour 2 litres of strawberry juice into fermenting vessel(s)

Strain cooled wort into fermenting vessel(s) and make up to 2 gallons with fresh water

Stir and take a sample for measurement of original gravity

Pitch 1g of ale yeast and 1g of sparkling wine or champagne yeast - fit an airlock

***

When fermentation is complete, allow the vessel to stand for a day or two to allow the brew to clear

When clear, rack into bottling bucket and batch prime with **64g** of brewing sugar
Transfer to 28 x 330ml bottles

Condition for two months at room temperature, then seven months at cellar temperature

Christmas Queen – Festive Triple Ale Mead

A friend described this as Christmas in a glass. It's essential to mature this, so try making some this year for next year's Christmas celebrations.

Batch size: Two Imperial Gallons   Expect: Original Gravity 1.084
                                     Final Gravity   1.004
                                     ABV   10.5%

Bring 8 litres of water to the boil

Add 25g of Hallertauer Hersbrucker hops – Boil for 25 minutes

Flame out

Add **6** x 454g of honey – Stir carefully to dissolve – Re-light the flame and bring back to the boil

Add 10 x crushed cloves, 10g of sliced fresh root ginger, 2 x cinnamon sticks and the carefully pared fresh zest from 4 medium oranges – Boil for 15 minutes

Add 15g of Hallertauer Mittelfrüh hops – Boil for 5 minutes

Flame out

Cool wort to 20°c or lower

Pour the juice of two oranges into the fermenting vessel(s) and add yeast nutrient

Strain cooled wort into fermenting vessel(s) and make up to 2 gallons with fresh water

Stir and take a sample for measurement of original gravity

Pitch 1g of ale yeast and 1g of sparkling wine or champagne yeast - fit an airlock

***

When fermentation is complete, allow the vessel to stand for a day or two to allow the brew to clear

When clear, rack into bottling bucket and batch prime with **64g** of brewing sugar
Transfer to 28 x 330ml bottles

Condition for two months at room temperature, then seven months at cellar temperature

BRAGGOTS

Ginger Queen – Light Ginger Braggot

Batch size: Two Imperial Gallons   Expect: Original Gravity 1.070
                                    Final Gravity   1.008
                                    ABV   8.1%

Heat 8 litres of water to 70°c and maintain temperature

Place 100g of light crystal malt in a muslin bag – Suspend the bag in the hot water and steep for 30 minutes

Remove malt bag

Add 1kg of light spray malt - Bring the wort to the boil

Add 20g of Hallertauer Hersbrucker hops – Boil for 25 minutes

Flame out

Add **2** x 454g of honey – Stir carefully to dissolve – Re-light the flame and bring back to the boil

Add 20g fresh sliced root ginger – Boil for 15 minutes

Add 10g of Hallertauer Mittelfrüh hops – Boil for 5 minutes

Flame out

Cool wort to 20°c or lower

Pour the juice of two oranges into the fermenting vessel(s) and add yeast nutrient

Strain cooled wort into fermenting vessel(s) and make up to 2 gallons with fresh water

Stir and take a sample for measurement of original gravity

Pitch 2g of ale yeast and fit an airlock

***

When fermentation is complete, allow the vessel to stand for a day or two to allow the brew to clear

When clear, rack into bottling bucket and batch prime with **64g** of brewing sugar
Transfer to 28 x 330ml bottles

Condition for two months at room temperature, then four months at cellar temperature

Bloody Mary – Light Cherry Braggot

Batch size: Two Imperial Gallons   Expect: Original Gravity 1.070
                                          Final Gravity   1.008
                                          ABV   8.1%

Heat 8 litres of water to 70°c and maintain temperature

Place 100g of light crystal malt in a muslin bag – Suspend the bag in the hot water and steep for 30 minutes

Remove malt bag

Add 1kg of light spray malt - Bring the wort to the boil

Add 20g of Hallertauer Hersbrucker hops – Boil for 25 minutes

Flame out

Add **2** x 454g of honey – Stir carefully to dissolve – Re-light the flame and bring back to the boil

Add 10g of Hallertauer Mittelfrüh hops – Boil for 5 minutes

Flame out

Cool wort to 20°c or lower

Pour the juice of two oranges into the fermenting vessel(s) and add yeast nutrient

Strain cooled wort into fermenting vessel(s) and make up to 2 gallons with fresh water

Stir and take a sample for measurement of original gravity

Add 1kg of fresh or frozen cherries – if using fresh fruit, wash under running water and slash the skins with a knife

Pitch 2g of ale yeast and fit an airlock

***

When fermentation is complete, allow the vessel to stand for a day or two to allow the brew to clear

When clear, rack into bottling bucket and batch prime with **64g** of brewing sugar
Transfer to 28 x 330ml bottles

Condition for two months at room temperature, then four months at cellar temperature

Lumber Jack – Light Maple Braggot

Batch size: Two Imperial Gallons

Expect: Original Gravity 1.075
Final Gravity 1.010
ABV 8.5%

Heat 8 litres of water to 70°c and maintain temperature

Place 100g of light crystal malt in a muslin bag – Suspend the bag in the hot water and steep for 30 minutes

Remove malt bag

Add 1kg of light spray malt - Bring the wort to the boil

Add 20g of Hallertauer Hersbrucker hops – Boil for 25 minutes

Flame out

Add **2** x 454g of honey – Stir carefully to dissolve – Re-light the flame and bring back to the boil

Add 10g of Hallertauer Mittelfrüh hops – Boil for 5 minutes

Add 250ml of pure maple syrup – Boil for 1 minute

Flame out

Cool wort to 20°c or lower

Pour the juice of two oranges into the fermenting vessel(s) and add yeast nutrient

Strain cooled wort into fermenting vessel(s) and make up to 2 gallons with fresh water

Stir and take a sample for measurement of original gravity

Pitch 2g of ale yeast and fit an airlock

***

When fermentation is complete, allow the vessel to stand for a day or two to allow the brew to clear

When clear, rack into bottling bucket and batch prime with **64g** of brewing sugar
Transfer to 28 x 330ml bottles

Condition for two months at room temperature, then four months at cellar temperature

Jack o' the Green – Light Greengage Braggot

I'm lucky enough to know a hedgerow which drips with wild greengage every autumn. But don't fret, most greengrocers carry greengage when they are in season. For a rounder, less tart product, you can use plums. Either way slash the skins with a knife and freeze the fruit for a few days before use.

Batch size: Two Imperial Gallons   Expect: Original Gravity 1.070
                                   Final Gravity   1.008
                                   ABV   8.1%

Heat 8 litres of water to 70°c and maintain temperature

Place 100g of light crystal malt in a muslin bag – Suspend the bag in the hot water and steep for 30 minutes

Remove malt bag

Add 1kg of light spray malt - Bring the wort to the boil

Add 20g of Hallertauer Hersbrucker hops – Boil for 25 minutes

Flame out

Add **2** x 454g of honey – Stir carefully to dissolve – Re-light the flame and bring back to the boil

Add 10g of Hallertauer Mittelfrüh hops – Boil for 5 minutes

Flame out

Cool wort to 20°c or lower

Pour the juice of two oranges into the fermenting vessel(s) and add yeast nutrient

Strain cooled wort into fermenting vessel(s) and make up to 2 gallons with fresh water

Stir and take a sample for measurement of original gravity

Add 2kg of greengage

Pitch 2g of ale yeast and fit an airlock

***

When fermentation is complete, allow the vessel to stand for a day or two to allow the brew to clear

When clear, rack into bottling bucket and batch prime with **64g** of brewing sugar
Transfer to 28 x 330ml bottles

Condition for two months at room temperature, then four months at cellar temperature

***

Variation: Substitute plums for the greengage

Hallowe'en Jack – Apple Wheat Braggot

Batch size: Two Imperial Gallons   Expect: Original Gravity 1.070
                                          Final Gravity   1.008
                                          ABV   8.1%

Heat 8 litres of water to 70°c and maintain temperature

Place 100g of light crystal malt in a muslin bag – Suspend the bag in the hot water and steep for 30 minutes

Remove malt bag

Add 1kg of wheat spray malt - Bring the wort to the boil

Add 20g of Hallertauer Hersbrucker hops – Boil for 25 minutes

Flame out

Add **2** x 454g of honey – Stir carefully to dissolve – Re-light the flame and bring back to the boil

Add 10g of Hallertauer Mittelfrüh hops – Boil for 5 minutes

Flame out

Cool wort to 20°c or lower

Pour the juice of two oranges into the fermenting vessel(s) and add yeast nutrient

Strain cooled wort into fermenting vessel(s) and make up to 2 gallons with fresh water

Stir and take a sample for measurement of original gravity

Add 12 x dessert apples and 2 x cooking apples, washed and sliced

Pitch 1g of ale yeast and 1g cider yeast - fit an airlock

***

When fermentation is complete, allow the vessel to stand for a day or two to allow the brew to clear

When clear, rack into bottling bucket and batch prime with **64g** of brewing sugar
Transfer to 28 x 330ml bottles

Condition for two months at room temperature, then four months at cellar temperature

Nelson's Victory – Medium Oaked Braggot

Batch size: Two Imperial Gallons   Expect: Original Gravity 1.070
                                     Final Gravity   1.008
                                     ABV   8.1%

Heat 8 litres of water to 70°c and maintain temperature

Place 100g of roasted barley in a muslin bag – Suspend the bag in the hot water and steep for 30 minutes

Remove malt bag

Add 1kg of medium spray malt - Bring the wort to the boil

Add 20g of Admiral hops – Boil for 25 minutes

Flame out

Add **2** x 454g of honey – Stir carefully to dissolve – Re-light the flame and bring back to the boil

Add 10g of Fuggles hops – Boil for 5 minutes

Flame out

Cool wort to 20°c or lower

Pour the juice of two oranges into the fermenting vessel(s) and add yeast nutrient

Place 4g of oak chips into the fermenting vessel(s)

Strain cooled wort into fermenting vessel(s) and make up to 2 gallons with fresh water

Stir and take a sample for measurement of original gravity

Pitch 2g of ale yeast and fit an airlock

***

When fermentation is complete, allow the vessel to stand for a day or two to allow the brew to clear

When clear, rack into bottling bucket and batch prime with **64g** of brewing sugar
Transfer to 28 x 330ml bottles

Condition for two months at room temperature, then four months at cellar temperature

Jack Tar – Dark Liquorice Braggot

Batch size: Two Imperial Gallons

Expect: Original Gravity 1.075
Final Gravity 1.010
ABV 8.5%

Heat 8 litres of water to 70°c and maintain temperature

Place 100g of black malt in a muslin bag – Suspend the bag in the hot water and steep for 30 minutes

Remove malt bag

Add 1kg of dark spray malt - Bring the wort to the boil

Add 20g of Goldings hops – Boil for 25 minutes

Flame out

Add **2** x 454g of honey – Stir carefully to dissolve – Re-light the flame and bring back to the boil

Add 10g chopped liquorice root – Boil for 15 minutes

Add 10g of Fuggles hops – Boil for 5 minutes

Flame out

Cool wort to 20°c or lower

Pour the juice of two oranges into the fermenting vessel(s) and add yeast nutrient

Strain cooled wort into fermenting vessel(s) and make up to 2 gallons with fresh water

Stir and take a sample for measurement of original gravity

Pitch 2g of ale yeast

***

When fermentation is complete, allow the vessel to stand for a day or two to allow the brew to clear

When clear, rack into bottling bucket and batch prime with **64g** of brewing sugar
Transfer to 28 x 330ml bottles

Condition for two months at room temperature, then four months at cellar temperature

DOUBLE BRAGGOTS

May Queen – Elderflower Double Light Braggot

Batch size: Two Imperial Gallons

Expect: Original Gravity 1.098
Final Gravity 1.018
ABV 10.5%

Heat 8 litres of water to 70°c and maintain temperature

Place 100g of light crystal malt in a muslin bag – Suspend the bag in the hot water and steep for 30 minutes

Remove malt bag

Add 1kg of light spray malt - Bring the wort to the boil

Add 20g of Hallertauer Hersbrucker hops – Boil for 25 minutes

Flame out

Add **4** x 454g of honey – Stir carefully to dissolve – Re-light the flame and bring back to the boil

Add 20g dried elderflower – Boil for 15 minutes

Add 10g of Hallertauer Mittelfrüh – Boil for 5 minutes

Flame out

Cool wort to 20°c or lower

Steep 10g dried elderflower in a small bowl of just-boiled water for 20 minutes – Strain the liquid into the fermenting vessel(s)

Pour the juice of two oranges into the fermenting vessel(s) and add yeast nutrient

Strain cooled wort into fermenting vessel(s) and make up to 2 gallons with fresh water

Stir and take a sample for measurement of original gravity

Pitch 2g of ale yeast

***

When fermentation is complete, allow the vessel to stand for a day or two to allow the brew to clear

When clear, rack into bottling bucket and batch prime with **64g** of brewing sugar
Transfer to 28 x 330ml bottles

Condition for two months at room temperature, then seven months at cellar temperature

***

Variation: Omit dried elderflower. De-stem three pints of freshly picked elderflowers and place in the bottom of the fermenting vessel(s) with the orange juice and nutrients. Do not cool the wort. Instead, carefully strain the just-boiled wort onto the elderflowers.
Close the vessel(s) under airlock while the wort cools naturally – this may take a few hours.
When the wort has cooled to 20°c or lower, stir and take a sample for measurement of original gravity, pitch the yeast and proceed as described above.

Wicker Man – Greengage Double Light Braggot

Slash the skins with a knife and freeze the fruit for a few days before use.

Batch size: Two Imperial Gallons   Expect: Original Gravity 1.098
                                    Final Gravity   1.018
                                    ABV   10.5%

Heat 8 litres of water to 70°c and maintain temperature

Place 100g of light crystal malt in a muslin bag – Suspend the bag in the hot water and steep for 30 minutes

Remove malt bag

Add 1kg of light spray malt - Bring the wort to the boil

Add 20g of Hallertauer Hersbrucker hops – Boil for 25 minutes

Flame out

Add **4** x 454g of honey – Stir carefully to dissolve – Re-light the flame and bring back to the boil

Add 10g of Hallertauer Mittelfrüh – Boil for 5 minutes

Flame out

Cool wort to 20°c or lower

Pour the juice of two oranges into the fermenting vessel(s) and add yeast nutrient

Strain cooled wort into fermenting vessel(s) and make up to 2 gallons with fresh water

Stir and take a sample for measurement of original gravity

Add 2kg of greengage

Pitch 2g of ale yeast

***

When fermentation is complete, allow the vessel to stand for a day or two to allow the brew to clear

When clear, rack into bottling bucket and batch prime with **64g** of brewing sugar
Transfer to 28 x 330ml bottles

Condition for two months at room temperature, then seven months at cellar temperature

***

Variation: Substitute plums for the greengage

Queen of Scots – Double Light Braggot

Plan ahead and soak your sultanas in whisky for at least a few weeks prior to brew day. By happy coincidence, 200g of sultanas fit nicely into an empty honey jar. Pour in enough whisky to cover the fruit and store in a cool, dark place. When you use the fruit, drain off the whisky into a glass and save it as a post-brew treat for when you've finished clearing up.

Batch size: Two Imperial Gallons

Expect: Original Gravity 1.098
Final Gravity 1.018
ABV 10.5%

Heat 8 litres of water to 70°c and maintain temperature

Place 100g of light crystal malt in a muslin bag – Suspend the bag in the hot water and steep for 30 minutes

Remove malt bag

Add 1kg of light spray malt - Bring the wort to the boil

Add 20g of Hallertauer Hersbrucker hops – Boil for 25 minutes

Flame out

Add **4** x 454g of honey – Stir carefully to dissolve – Re-light the flame and bring back to the boil

Add 10g of Hallertauer Mittelfrüh – Boil for 5 minutes

Flame out

Cool wort to 20°c or lower

Pour the juice of two oranges into the fermenting vessel(s) and add yeast nutrient

Strain cooled wort into fermenting vessel(s) and make up to 2 gallons with fresh water

Stir and take a sample for measurement of original gravity

Add 200g of whisky-soaked sultanas. Drain the whisky from the sultanas and add the fruit (not the whisky) to the fermenting vessel(s)

Pitch 1g of ale yeast and 1g of sparkling wine yeast

***

When fermentation is complete, allow the vessel to stand for a day or two to allow the brew to clear

When clear, rack into bottling bucket and batch prime with **64g** of brewing sugar
Transfer to 28 x 330ml bottles

Condition for two months at room temperature, then seven months at cellar temperature

Gun Decks – Double Dark Braggot

Plan ahead and soak your raisins in dark rum for at least a few weeks prior to brew day. By happy coincidence, 200g of raisins fit nicely into an empty honey jar. Pour in enough dark rum to cover the fruit and store in a cool, dark place. When you use the fruit, drain off the rum into a glass and save it as a post-brew treat for when you've finished clearing up.

Batch size: Two Imperial Gallons

Expect: Original Gravity 1.098
Final Gravity 1.018
ABV 10.5%

Heat 8 litres of water to 70°c and maintain temperature

Place 100g of black malt in a muslin bag – Suspend the bag in the hot water and steep for 30 minutes

Remove malt bag

Add 1kg of dark spray malt - Bring the wort to the boil

Add 20g of Goldings hops – Boil for 25 minutes

Flame out

Add **4** x 454g of honey – Stir carefully to dissolve – Re-light the flame and bring back to the boil

Add 10g of Fuggles – Boil for 5 minutes

Flame out

Cool wort to 20°c or lower

Pour the juice of two oranges into the fermenting vessel(s) and add yeast nutrient

Strain cooled wort into fermenting vessel(s) and make up to 2 gallons with fresh water

Stir and take a sample for measurement of original gravity

Add 200g of rum-soaked raisins. Drain the rum from the raisins and add the fruit (not the rum) to the fermenting vessel(s)

Pitch 1g of ale yeast and 1g of sparkling wine yeast

***

When fermentation is complete, allow the vessel to stand for a day or two to allow the brew to clear

When clear, rack into bottling bucket and batch prime with **64g** of brewing sugar
Transfer to 28 x 330ml bottles

Condition for two months at room temperature, then seven months at cellar temperature

SESSION BRAGGOTS

Black Jack – Extra Dark Session Braggot

Batch size: Three-and-a-half Imperial Gallons

Expect: Original Gravity 1.040
Final Gravity 1.006
ABV 4.5%

Heat 8 litres of water to 70°c and maintain temperature

Place 100g of black malt and 100g of roasted barley in a muslin bag – Suspend the bag in the hot water and steep for 30 minutes

Remove malt bag

Add 1kg of extra dark spray malt - Bring the wort to the boil

Add 30g of Goldings hops – Boil for 25 minutes

Flame out

Add **2** x 454g of honey – Stir carefully to dissolve – Re-light the flame and bring back to the boil

Add 20g of chopped liquorice root – Boil for 15 minutes

Add 15g of Fuggles – Boil for 5 minutes

Flame out

Cool wort to 20°c or lower

Pour the juice of three oranges into the fermenting vessel(s) and add yeast nutrient

Strain cooled wort into fermenting vessel(s) and make up to three-and-one-half gallons with fresh water

Stir and take a sample for measurement of original gravity

Pitch 3g of ale yeast

***

When fermentation is complete, allow the vessel to stand for a day or two to allow the brew to clear

When clear, rack into bottling bucket and batch prime with **95g** of brewing sugar
Transfer to 32 x 500ml bottles

Condition for two months at room temperature

Ginger Tom – Light Session Braggot

Batch size: Three-and-one-half Imperial Gallons

Expect: Original Gravity	1.040
Final Gravity	1.006
ABV	4.5%

Heat 8 litres of water to 70°c and maintain temperature

Place 100g of light crystal malt in a muslin bag – Suspend the bag in the hot water and steep for 30 minutes

Remove malt bag

Add 1kg of light spray malt - Bring the wort to the boil

Add 20g of Admiral hops – Boil for 25 minutes

Flame out

Add **2** x 454g of honey – Stir carefully to dissolve – Re-light the flame and bring back to the boil

Add 30g of sliced fresh ginger and 30g of dried elderflower – Boil for 15 minutes

Add 15g of Amarillo hops – Boil for 5 minutes

Flame out

Cool wort to 20°c or lower

Steep 15g dried elderflower in a small bowl of just-boiled water for 20 minutes – Strain the liquid into the fermenting vessel(s)

Pour the juice of three oranges into the fermenting vessel(s) and add yeast nutrient

Strain cooled wort into fermenting vessel(s) and make up to three-and-one-half gallons with fresh water

Stir and take a sample for measurement of original gravity

Pitch 3g of ale yeast

***

When fermentation is complete, allow the vessel to stand for a day or two to allow the brew to clear

When clear, rack into bottling bucket and batch prime with **95g** of brewing sugar
Transfer to 32 x 500ml bottles

Condition for two months at room temperature

***

Variation: Omit dried elderflower. De-stem three pints of freshly picked elderflowers and place in the bottom of the fermenting vessel(s) with the orange juice and nutrients. Do not cool the wort. Instead, carefully strain the just-boiled wort onto the elderflowers.
Close the vessel(s) under airlock while the wort cools naturally – this may take a few hours.
When the wort has cooled to 20°c or lower, stir and take a sample for measurement of original gravity, pitch the yeast and proceed as described above.
For a cleaner ginger finish, omit the elderflower completely.

Green Man – Greengage Light Session Braggot

Slash the skins with a knife and freeze the fruit for a few days before use.

Batch size: Three-and-one-half Imperial Gallons

    Expect: Original Gravity 1.040
    Final Gravity   1.006
    ABV   4.5%

Heat 8 litres of water to 70°c and maintain temperature

Place 100g of light crystal malt in a muslin bag – Suspend the bag in the hot water and steep for 30 minutes

Remove malt bag

Add 1kg of light spray malt - Bring the wort to the boil

Add 30g of Hallertauer Hersbrucker hops – Boil for 25 minutes

Flame out

Add **2** x 454g of honey – Stir carefully to dissolve – Re-light the flame and bring back to the boil

Add 15g of Hallertauer Mittelfrüh – Boil for 5 minutes

Flame out

Cool wort to 20°c or lower

Pour the juice of three oranges into the fermenting vessel(s) and add yeast nutrient

Strain cooled wort into fermenting vessel(s) and make up to three-and-one-half gallons with fresh water

Stir and take a sample for measurement of original gravity

Add 3kg of greengage

Pitch 3g of ale yeast

***

When fermentation is complete, allow the vessel to stand for a day or two to allow the brew to clear

When clear, rack into bottling bucket and batch prime with **95g** of brewing sugar
Transfer to 32 x 500ml bottles

Condition for two months at room temperature

***

Variation: Substitute plums for the greengage

Jack Bracket – Apple Light Session Braggot

Bracket is another name that was often used for Braggot

Batch size: Three-and-one-half Imperial Gallons

> Expect: Original Gravity 1.040
> Final Gravity 1.006
> ABV 4.5%

Heat 8 litres of water to 70°c and maintain temperature

Place 100g of light crystal malt in a muslin bag – Suspend the bag in the hot water and steep for 30 minutes

Remove malt bag

Add 1kg of light spray malt - Bring the wort to the boil

Add 30g of Hallertauer Hersbrucker hops – Boil for 25 minutes

Flame out

Add **2** x 454g of honey – Stir carefully to dissolve – Re-light the flame and bring back to the boil

Add 15g of Hallertauer Mittelfrüh – Boil for 5 minutes

Flame out

Cool wort to 20°c or lower

Pour the juice of three oranges into the fermenting vessel(s) and add yeast nutrient

Strain cooled wort into fermenting vessel(s) and make up to three-and-one-half gallons with fresh water

Stir and take a sample for measurement of original gravity

Add 18 x dessert apples and 3 x cooking apples, washed and sliced

Pitch 3g of ale yeast

***

When fermentation is complete, allow the vessel to stand for a day or two to allow the brew to clear

When clear, rack into bottling bucket and batch prime with **95g** of brewing sugar
Transfer to 32 x 500ml bottles

Condition for two months at room temperature

Carnival Queen – Elderflower Wheat Session Braggot

Batch size: Three-and-one-half Imperial Gallons

Expect: Original Gravity 1.040
Final Gravity 1.006
ABV 4.5%

Heat 8 litres of water to 70°c and maintain temperature

Place 100g of light crystal malt in a muslin bag – Suspend the bag in the hot water and steep for 30 minutes

Remove malt bag

Add 1kg of wheat spray malt - Bring the wort to the boil

Add 30g of Hallertauer Hersbrucker hops – Boil for 25 minutes

Flame out

Add **2** x 454g of honey – Stir carefully to dissolve – Re-light the flame and bring back to the boil

Add 30g dried elderflower – Boil for 15 minutes

Add 15g of Hallertauer Mittelfrüh – Boil for 5 minutes

Flame out

Cool wort to 20°c or lower

Steep 15g dried elderflower in a small bowl of just-boiled water for 20 minutes – Strain the liquid into the fermenting vessel(s)

Pour the juice of three oranges into the fermenting vessel(s) and add yeast nutrient

Strain cooled wort into fermenting vessel(s) and make up to three-and-one-half gallons with fresh water

Stir and take a sample for measurement of original gravity

Pitch 3g of ale yeast

***

When fermentation is complete, allow the vessel to stand for a day or two to allow the brew to clear

When clear, rack into bottling bucket and batch prime with **95g** of brewing sugar
Transfer to 32 x 500ml bottles

Condition for two months at room temperature

***

Variation: Omit dried elderflower. De-stem four pints of freshly picked elderflowers and place in the bottom of the fermenting vessel(s) with the orange juice and nutrients. Do not cool the wort. Instead, carefully strain the just-boiled wort onto the elderflowers.
Close the vessel(s) under airlock while the wort cools naturally – this may take a few hours.
When the wort has cooled to 20°c or lower, stir and take a sample for measurement of original gravity, pitch the yeast and proceed as described above.

The Nelson Touch – Medium Rum and Cloves Session Braggot

Put 24 whole cloves in an egg-cup or similarly small container and cover with a small amount of dark rum for several days.

Batch size: Three-and-one-half Imperial Gallons

> Expect: Original Gravity 1.040
> Final Gravity 1.006
> ABV 4.5%

Heat 8 litres of water to 70°c and maintain temperature

Place 100g of light crystal malt in a muslin bag – Suspend the bag in the hot water and steep for 30 minutes

Remove malt bag

Add 1kg of medium spray malt - Bring the wort to the boil

Add 20g of Admiral hops – Boil for 25 minutes

Flame out

Add **2** x 454g of honey – Stir carefully to dissolve – Re-light the flame and bring back to the boil

Add 15g of Fuggles hops – Boil for 5 minutes

Flame out

Cool wort to 20°c or lower

Pour the juice of three oranges into the fermenting vessel(s) and add yeast nutrient

Strain cooled wort into fermenting vessel(s) and make up to three-and-one-half gallons with fresh water

Stir and take a sample for measurement of original gravity

Add 24 rum-soaked cloves to the fermenting vessel(s)

Pitch 3g of ale yeast

***

When fermentation is complete, allow the vessel to stand for a day or two to allow the brew to clear

When clear, rack into bottling bucket and batch prime with **95g** of brewing sugar
Transfer to 32 x 500ml bottles

Condition for two months at room temperature

YOUR BREWING NOTES

Brew number 1

Name of brew:
Out-turn:
Date bottled:
Date ready:

Brew number 2

Name of brew:
Out-turn:
Date bottled:
Date ready:

Brew number 3

Name of brew:
Out-turn:
Date bottled:
Date ready:

Brew number 4

Name of brew:
Out-turn:
Date bottled:
Date ready:

Brew number 5

Name of brew:
Out-turn:
Date bottled:
Date ready:

Brew number 6

Name of brew:
Out-turn:
Date bottled:
Date ready:

Brew number 7

Name of brew:
Out-turn:
Date bottled:
Date ready:

Brew number 8

Name of brew:
Out-turn:
Date bottled:
Date ready:

Brew number 9

Name of brew:
Out-turn:
Date bottled:
Date ready:

Brew number 10

Name of brew:
Out-turn:
Date bottled:
Date ready:

Brew number 11

Name of brew:
Out-turn:
Date bottled:
Date ready:

Brew number 12

Name of brew:
Out-turn:
Date bottled:
Date ready:

Brew number 13

Name of brew:
Out-turn:
Date bottled:
Date ready:

Brew number 14

Name of brew:
Out-turn:
Date bottled:
Date ready:

Brew number 15

Name of brew:
Out-turn:
Date bottled:
Date ready:

Brew number 16

Name of brew:
Out-turn:
Date bottled:
Date ready:

Brew number 17

Name of brew:
Out-turn:
Date bottled:
Date ready:

Brew number 18

Name of brew:
Out-turn:
Date bottled:
Date ready:

Brew number 19

Name of brew:
Out-turn:
Date bottled:
Date ready:

Brew number 20

Name of brew:
Out-turn:
Date bottled:
Date ready:

www.ingramcontent.com/pod-product-compliance
Lightning Source LLC
Chambersburg PA
CBHW060340050426
42449CB00011B/2799